Beauty of

Washington

Beauty of

Washington

Text: Paul M. Lewis
Concept & Design: Robert D. Shangle

First Printing January, 1989
Published by LTA Publishing Company
1425 S.E. 18th Avenue, Portland, Oregon 97214
Robert D. Shangle, Publisher

"Learn about America in a beautiful way."

Library of Congress Cataloging-in-Publication Data

Beauty of Washington
/concept & design, Robert D. Shangle; text, Paul M. Lewis.
      p.   cm.
ISBN 0-917630-64-5; $19.95. — ISBN 0-917630-63-7 (pbk.); $9.95
    1. Washington (state) — Description and travel — 1981 — Views.
I. Shangle, Robert D. II. Lewis, Paul M.
F892.B4   1989   88-37211
917.97'0443 — dc19   CIP

Contents

Introduction

When I was a kid growing up in Philadelphia, I never spent much time wondering about the country west of the Monongahela River. I realized in a vague sort of way that the world did not end at the western borders of Pennsylvania, but that part of the country beyond the Rockies was as unknown to me as the heart of darkest Africa. When I reached the age of wisdom — about 14, I think — I began to grow aware of the West Coast. Al Jolson was singing a song called "California, Here I Come" about that time. For a while I was under the impression that the Pacific Coast began and ended with California.

I have lived for some 30 years in the Pacific Northwest, a region my peers and I thought was pure myth while we were all still exploring the wilds of North Philadelphia. In our very circumscribed world, the *real* Washington was that city two-and-a-half hours away on the Pennsy, where Philadelphia school kids went to see the United States Capitol and the Lincoln Memorial. The State of Washington was one of those wilderness places out west somewhere, covered with ice and snow and full of Indians and grizzly bears. We regarded it as something of an interloper, because *our* Washington had been there first.

Interloper or not, Washington State has long since been admitted to the union by us eastern establishment types. In some ways it is still very close to the naive idea I had of it as a child. Parts of it *are* covered with ice and snow. Indian tribes live in other parts. And there must be a few grizzly bears somewhere in all those woods.

The main trouble with my childish imaginings is that they didn't go far enough. The Evergreen State contains far greater wonders than those constructed out of my undernourished fantasies. It's a smallish state by western standards, not nearly so big as its neighbors in the northwest corner of the country. But within its borders, as any Washingtonian will inform you, is more scenic variety than any other state can claim. A brag like this may at first seem more challenge than reality, considering the range of natural features scattered over the 50 United States.

One way to settle the matter is with a book like this, where page after page of magnificent color portraits attest to Washington's kaleidoscopic beauty. Every part of the state is represented, its matchless settings copied with remarkable fidelity.

For starters, there's the coast. On the south are long, low sandy beaches. To the north, on the Olympic Peninsula, massive cliffs and headlands cut through the beaches, and the near shore is riddled with free-standing rocks and pinnacles.

The peninsula's interior is a separate story. In an area about 70 miles square are violent differences in climate and topography. The intricate and rugged mass of the Olympic Moutains presents a close-knit circle of glaciated peaks; on the windward side of the mountains are the lush rain forests of Olympic National Park, where prodigal rains and mild temperatures produce outsize plant growth. In the lee of the Olympics, on the peninsula's north coast, is a trough of mild, dry air about 20-miles wide where rainfall averages only 14 inches a year.

Consider Puget Sound, a unique blending of landscape and seascape with its infinite patterns and relationships.

Then there are the North Cascades, Washington's end of the long, high chain of mountains that are weather systems in themselves, controlling much of what happens on the east side of the state. These jumbled northern giants, together, make up a rugged wilderness area that is without parallel in the rest of the country, excepting Alaska.

On the east slope of the Cascades, the productive Wenatchee and Yakima valleys provide agricultural bounty for farmers and orchardists. The northern Okanogan Highlands embrace some "Texas-style" cattle ranches and some old mining towns; the towns are relics of the last century's gold fever. To the south, the Columbia Basin region yields a variety of crops with the help of Grand Coulee and other giant dams.

In the southeast corner, the landscape takes on yet another character. Here are fertile valleys, semi-desert lands, barren mountains, canyons, coulees, and deep gorges cut by rivers the likes of the Snake and the Palouse.

So whatever the world's temperate zone has to offer in climate and natural features, Washington includes most of the variations. From the human point of view, the state runs the gamut: it's hot, cold, damp, dry, ruggedly mountainous, and serenely pastoral. Washington's wide range of climatic zones and terrains support an extraordinary variety of plant and animal species.

These days we seem to be altering our mental set about the natural world. We are gradually being weaned from the notion that nature is "out there." To paraphrase the late cartoonist, Walt Kelley, "We have looked at nature, and it is us." We seem to be more aware of the interaction of all natural things and of our special responsibilities toward the places where we live. Washingtonians, like other Americans who live in the midst of beauty, are deeply committed to preserving their state's natural riches so that succeeding generations may inherit its treasure-house of blessings.

P.M.L.

Puget Sound

All of us have, at one time or another, imagined we were in a far-off land, perhaps living on a tiny island in a calm sea, which is dotted with other islands close enough to be friendly but not close enough to be nosy. Some of the islands are entirely covered with thick evergreen forests, while others front the water with steep cliffs, secret coves, or low, sandy beaches. All around the horizon is spectacular scenery, mostly mountain ranges raising glaciated spires to the sky. At night, in our imaginings, we see several glowing points on the horizon that must be cities — one of the light areas, to the south, is especially impressive. We're glad our island world can be so remote from, while yet so near to, those crowded-together people places.

Too bad we're dreaming, we might say in our dream. But to anyone who has ever been to Puget Sound, especially in the north Sound where the San Juan Islands lie, this is real. Fortunately, Puget Sound really exists, improbable as that may seem. This inland sea, with its hundreds of islands, multitudes of waterways, harbors, coves, inlets, and shores, has a miraculous beauty that is all the more amazing for its being next door to the most densely populated area in the Northwest, the Seattle-Tacoma metropolitan complex. In fact the major proportion of Washington State's population is encamped on the shores of the Sound. Nearly all of the big cities have their feet in its waters — for instance, Olympia, Tacoma, Seattle, Bremerton, Everett and Bellingham.

A map of the Sound can only give an approximation of the complicated stew of land and waterways that make up this unique part of the world. The Kitsap Peninsula, itself saved from island status only by a narrow neck of land near its base, bulges importantly over much of the lower Sound. Hood Canal slices between it and the Olympic Peninsula on the west, and the Sound proper separates it from the east shore. Kitsap has a wealth of fishing ports and natural attractions related to its land-sea ambience. Its major city is Bremerton, of Navy Yard fame.

The Puget Sound's "highways" are the ferry routes with their fleets of auto-carrying ferries that sail the inland seas between the cities of the east shore — Seattle, Tacoma, Everett, and the Kitsap and Olympic peninsulas, thirteen islands, and Vancouver Island. Ferry travel through these waters, with their variety of landscapes and harbors, is a rich experience, indeed. The ferry rides are sufficient unto themselves even with no car along to take you somewhere at the end of the voyage.

The best-known parcels of real estate here are the San Juan Islands. Strictly speaking, they aren't even in the Sound, which officially includes only the southern portion, beginning with the entrance to Hood Canal. But the San Juans are popularly considered to be a part of it. They number 172 big and little islands and are scattered all over the northern arm of the inland sea. Ferries carry people and things to some of these islands. The best-known trip by ferry is the one between Anacortes, Washington, and Sidney, B.C. The three-hour route slips through the islands and visits some of the small ports on Lopez, Shaw, Orcas, and San Juan islands. Private boats or charter boats are, of course, other means of transportation around the San Juans. One of the fascinations of the islands is their impression of remoteness, even though they're not remote in the matter of distance. Many of them are uninhabited and some are for sale.

The thorough exploration of the San Juans would require more than a lifetime of looking by a dedicated mariner. But that does not deter the weekend sailor, who can usually find a snug, secluded harbor to suit his fancy, wherever in the islands his wanderlust leads him. There is no commercial development of any consequence, although resorts are plentiful. The facilities offered are of the modest, cottage type. A popular summer evening pastime is the beach picnic, with driftwood fires, clam bakes, and fish suppers.

The biggest of the San Juans is Orcas Island. It has a comfortable, resort atmosphere, with settlements around the island connected by paved roads. For the tourist there are campsites, boating, swimming, and fishing in Moran State

Park. The highest point in the San Juans is on Orcas (Mt. Constitution — 2,409 feet), which commands a full-circle view of the other islands.

San Juan Island is the most populated. Its city, Friday Harbor, is also the county seat of San Juan County, which includes most of the San Juan group. This island once had its troubles with the Indians, and some of the blockhouses built during this time are still standing. Its most memorable moment in history came in 1859 when it was the site of the "pig war," a comic-opera dispute between the Americans and the British over who owned the island. It began when an American settler shot a pig that belonged to an Englishman, riling the (British) authorities. The American called for help, and both Americans and British landed troops (100 each, by agreement). In the years that followed, the garrisons whiled away the idle time by throwing parties and giving banquets for each other, until, in 1872, the German emperor, as arbitrator, awarded the San Juans to the United States.

Puget Sound is also a big lumber country — off the water, of course. The ample rainfall makes the Douglas Fir grow 200-feet tall and four to six feet in diameter. While the loggers don't actually drop the trees from the banks to the water, the accessibility of the inland sea makes transportation a relatively simple affair. Hood Canal is a busy waterway for the transport of logs from the forests of the Olympic Peninsula. They are formed into rafts which are taken in tow by tugs. Brands, similar to cattle brands, are used to identify logs in case a raft breaks up.

The complicated land-sea interplay that is Puget Sound may some day be changed by slow-working natural forces into something that has little resemblance to the Sound of today. That will probably not happen before thousands, or even hundreds of thousands of years pass. One natural force that can radically and quickly alter the nature of this fantastic fairyland of island-strewn inland waterways is man. Our power to manipulate our surroundings poses an especially serious threat in a setting where intricate relationships require a light touch. So far the record is good, and the Sound has escaped the heavy-handed development characteristic of some other recreation areas in this country.

Olympic Peninsula

Because the Olympic Peninsula is such a variety of things, it's quite impossible to characterize briefly. To make things easier, the Olympic coastal strip has been discussed in the chapter dealing with the state's coastline. The obvious preliminary things to say about this land mass concern its size and shape. On the map its squarish contour looks something like a thumb or big toe appended to the body of the country. Distances are moderate; the peninsula is about 75 miles east-to-west at its widest point and the same from the northern tip to Grays Harbor at its base. It is bordered on the east by Hood Canal, on the north by the Strait of Juan de Fuca, and on the west by the Pacific Ocean.

US Highway 101 makes a neat loop around the peninsula, following the coast along the eastern side and as far as Port Angeles on the north. But then, as if distracted by its proximity to the superlative Olympic Mountains, it heads inland and for a time skirts the national park containing these craggy peaks. Although avoiding the coast for most of the rest of its circuit, it stays close enough to the perimeter to enclose most of the peninsula's variety.

The road takes off from Olympia, Washington's capital, and begins its meandering route along the wooded shore of Hood Canal. Along the 30 miles of the canal are fishing resorts and gravel beaches, popular with clam diggers (when the weather is right). Spur roads in this stretch lead up steep river valleys of the Hamma Hamma, Duckabush, and Dosewallips rivers that flow down from the Olympic mountains.

At the northeastern corner of the peninsula is Discovery Bay, named in 1792 by the English sea captain, George Vancouver, after his ship. Following a side road on the Bay's eastern shore, we come to Port Townsend, on the extreme northeast tip of a finger of land edged by the bay and Puget Sound. Port

Townsend has distinction as a kind of architectural museum, where the Victorian buildings have been preserved and restored. The town has been "frozen" to look about the way it did in the last century, when it was the most important entrance to the Sound.

Farther west is Port Angeles, the peninsula's largest town and lumber center for the north peninsula. Its excellent natural harbor, protected on the west by a narrow sliver of land, accommodates ocean freighters, mostly for loading with export logs. Port Angeles is also the main northern entrance to Olympic National Park. From here Hurricane Ridge highway takes a scenic course for 13 miles up to Hurricane Ridge Lodge on Big Meadow. At the lodge the closeup panorama of the Olympics is a show-stopper and a tourist-stopper. Lordly Mt. Olympus is center stage, standing above the jumbled mass of the peaks on its flanks. The ridge road goes through dense forests along the way to Big Meadow and Obstruction Point, farther along. Occasional viewpoints allow the traveler to look down on Port Angeles, northeast to the San Juan Islands and Mt. Baker, and, on the very top of the ridge, to take in all the inner Olympics.

Olympic National Park was dedicated as a wilderness in 1946, which means that it has remained in its natural state. West of Port Angeles, US 101 brushes its northern edge briefly, but no roads cross the mountains, although some spur roads go up the valleys. But it is one of the easiest wildernesses to penetrate and enjoy, if one is willing to do it on foot. The park has at least three distinct regions: the north, west, and east. The north contains some of the best woodland, the biggest lake (Lake Crescent), spectacular alpine meadows, and the heaviest snowfall.

The west, or "wet" side, including the coastal strip, recieves up to 150 inches of rain annually from clouds that pile up against the mountains, after having been driven in on prevailing southwest Pacific winds. Here is where the trees grow to colossal size in a rain forest that is unique on the face of the earth. Everything is mantled in moss and the undergrowth is extremely dense. Rain forests don't grow different species of plants from other forests — every growing thing just does it more exuberantly and in a bigger way. Open spaces on the forest floor are kept so in part by the browsing of the famed Olympic elk. But even in this dense, jungle-like environment, the forest is far from gloomy. A soft, green light filters through and is reflected by the leaves and mosses. The Bogachiel and Hoh River valleys contain some of the best examples of rain forest, and trails through these forests are very popular with hikers.

The southeast side of the wilderness is the "dry" part, in comparison with the rain forest. This area is notable for its dense forests of fir, cedar, and hemlock, and for its steep, narrow river valleys.

Once the highway has curved around the Olympic National Park it has nearly finished its odyssey on the peninsula. Before bending sharply inland and shooting straight south for Hoquiam-Aberdeen at the peninsula's base, the road cuts through 11 miles of the park's coastal strip.

On the north coast are some places of interest looking out on the Strait of Juan de Fuca. West, along the coast from Port Angeles, State Highway 112 sometimes rides high over the strait, sometimes stays level with the beach. Along the way to the northwest tip of the peninsula, it passes tree farms, fishing villages, and lumber towns. Sekiu, near Neah Bay, is home to a whole fleet of boats that crowd its bay when the salmon are migrating from ocean to river. Here, big log rafts are made up in a technique called "booming" and are towed by tug to mills. Neah Bay, at the end of the highway, has been an Indian fishing town since long before the white man's arrival. Commercial fishing fleets are active in the summer here, but disappear in the winter, when Neah Bay is buffeted by the stormy ocean. Cape Flattery, at the very tip, is at the end of a six-mile road from Neah Bay plus a one-mile hike. From the high ground of the cape, there's a splendid view of the pounding ocean and of solitary Tatoosh Island with its lighthouse.

An excursion into the wilds of the Olympics or around the other parts of the Olympic Peninsula leaves the traveler with a sense of wonder and gratitude. Wonder at the lavish hand of nature in fashioning so much beauty. Gratitude that we seem to be learning our responsibilities in caring for such beauty.

The Coast

The side of Washington that faces the Pacific is at least two-faced. More accurately, many-faced. The coastline is about two-thirds Olympic Peninsula coast and one-third Washington's south coast, if we consider just the shoreline that fronts the Pacific Ocean. But Washington is never that simple, and emphatically not in the matter of coastlines. The northern segment, or what is called the Olympic seashore, goes from one point to another without a great many detours. It is measurable by counting the miles — about 100 from Cape Flattery to the North Bay of Grays Harbor. But along the lower coast, the Pacific has in effect taken two big swallows of shoreline and created Grays Harbor and Willapa Bay — the Twin Harbors, as they are called. If we add to the coastal mileage the enormous stretches of shoreline contained in these two extensive inlets, the distance is about equal to the northern, or the Olympic, part.

South of Cape Flattery is Point of Arches, one of the most beautiful parts of the entire coast. Rocks and rock islets are scattered in profusion offshore, many having been tunneled through by the incessant crashing of the waves. Tidepools and arches can be reached at low tide. Cape Alava, a few miles south, is the westernmost point in the three Pacific Coast states. At high tide it beats out Cape Flattery for that honor by a few hundred feet. At low tide it gives up the title to a small island linked to the mainland by a sandspit. The Island, named Indian, or Cannonball Island, has "cannonball" rocks whose spherical shape has not been completely explained by scientists. Cape Alava is the recipient, even more than other coastal "catch basins," of an enormous amount of lumber and other materials cast up by the sea.

Cape Alava, like many parts of this coast, has no roads leading to it. It is reached by four miles of trails from the end of the road at Ozette. The cape is also

Paradise River

Sunset from Mt. Young, San Juan Island

Whistler Mountain near Rainy Pass

Mt. Bonanza

Hoh Rain Forest

San Juan County Park, San Juan Island

Mt. Adams

Tacoma Narrows Bridge

Columbia River Gorge

Mt. St. Helens from the South

Steamboat Rock and Banks Lake

Elliot Bay, Seattle and Mt. Rainier

State Capitol Building, Olympia

The Space Needle, Seattle

Looking South from Mt. Young, San Juan Island

Cape Disappointment Lighthouse

Mt. Shuksan

Skagit River

Point of Arches, South of Neah Bay

Mt. Rainier and Reflection Lake

Looking East to Mt. Baker from Mt. Constitution, Orcas Island

Fort Vancouver

Roche Harbor, San Juan Island

Port Angeles Harbor

University of Washington, Seattle

Deception Pass, Whidbey Island

Ballooning over Walla Walla Valley

Eastern Washington Farming

Tulip Farm near Mossyrock

Eastern Washington Wheat Harvest

Goode Mountain

Long Beach

Snagtooth Ridge from Washington Pass

Dry Falls

Soleduck Falls

Ruby Beach, North of Kalaloch

Near Liberty

Lake Crescent

Near Wishram

Coastline north of Quetts

Diablo Lake

Bowman Bay, Deception Pass, Whidbey Island

Palouse River Canyon

Rosario Bay, Orcas Island

Palouse Falls

Gray River Covered Bridge

Ruby Beach

Sunset from North Beach, Deception Pass, Whidbey Island

at the northern end of the Olympic National Park's coastal strip, where dense forests and steep headlands south to Rialto Beach (17 miles) make hiking a reasonable venture only for the experienced and well prepared. At Rialto Beach and La Push the beach is reached by a road. La Push, on the Quillayute Indian Reservation, is a fishing village that caters to tourists, renting charter boats for salmon fishing and offering Indian articles for sale. The wilderness beach, itself, is flat and easily traveled on foot, except for the headlands encountered now and then. But beach hikers need to have a wary knowledge of high and low tides and to be on the watch for severe weather conditions.

Toleak Point, six miles south of La Push, is easily reached by hikers and is popular as a wilderness site. Three headlands are encountered along the way, but two of them can be skirted at low tide. At high tide they must be climbed. Trails are well marked and the scenery is as varied as it is on the beach. Toleak Point is a sanctuary for bald eagles, one of the few places outside of Alaska where these majestic birds thrive.

Down the coast through the Olympic strip are the Hoh River and the Hoh Indian Reservation. The Hoh River valley is a magnificent example of rain forest. Ruby Beach, a little way to the south, is the northern point where Highway 101 reaches out to the coast of the Olympic Peninsula and hugs it for 11 miles, the only part of the coast that is visited by this "Olympic loop" road. This strip is usually explored in short hikes from automobile starting points on the highway. In spite of the presence of the road, there are few signs of civilization. Offshore pinnacles and stacks, and tideland wilderness are the same as they were when no white man had seen them. Queets, at the southern end of the shoreside stretch of road, is an Indian village on the northern edge of the Quinault Indian Reservation. Access to the reservation is regulated by the Indians. The Quinault region is best for seeing the rain forest by car, because US Highway 101 goes through it. There are plenty of trails for those who still prefer more intimate exploration.

Past the Quinault area is a series of small communities that qualify as beach resorts. After the wilderness coast the scene has changed to the more familiar "managed" beaches, beautiful, flat, sandy stretches with tourist facilities. Clamming is popular here and is excellent all the way down to Grays Harbor. The south coast, with its twins, Grays and Willapa, is the land of summer resorts. Both harbors are guarded by narrow fingers of land. North Beach Peninsula's 28 miles of sand beach forms the skinny arm of Willapa Bay. More familiarly called Long Beach, this knife-blade sand spit has long been a popular vacation area for Portlanders, who came to Ilwaco by steamboat during the 1890s, taking a narrow gauge railroad to reach the resort towns strung along the beach. Even in winter the peninsula's long beaches are inviting. A road now connects the towns of the peninsula, but no through road reaches this long sand spit. One of Washington's oldest towns — Oysterville — is here. It has some buildings dating from the 1860s.

Willapa Bay is home to a lot of oysters, raised on private oyster farms. Grayland, midway between the harbors, has long been a cranberry growing center, from the time some early Finnish growers established the first bogs. The state highways on the middle coast include Grays Harbor in their routes: 109 follows the shore and 105 goes along the south harbor, reaching over to Willapa Bay's north shore. So the Twin Harbors are easy to explore by car, especially since US 101 roams the east and south shores of Willapa.

This summary tour of Washington's inimitable coastline can only whet the appetite for a taste of the real thing. Until one can be there, physically, he may derive considerable pleasure from a look at some facsimiles — the photographic images spread out in the pages of this book. The sample of the coast represented in our galaxy of Washington scenes may help to remind us of all the wonderful and beautiful things on this earth that have nothing to do with our presence here. Washington's coast symbolizes nature's complex design, of which we are just one aspect.

Southern Washington

If there really is a southern Washington, it must be that part of the state along the Columbia, the part whose rivers and streams drain directly into that immense trough. For convenience we have so designated this general region, because to stray very far north at any point along the river is to identify with another part of the state.

The town of Ilwaco is just inside the rough waters of the mouth of the Columbia. If one drives the 200 miles from Ilwaco to Horse Heaven Hills, the pace is much slower than on the Oregon side, where a super-duper highway zips the motorist past all the sumptuous scenery before he has had time to look at it. The headlands at the mouth are rugged and forested, but excellent viewpoints to watch freighters getting tossed around while crossing the Columbia River bar. This stormy meeting of the waters has brought to grief hundreds of ships, some of whose remains can still be seen sinking into the sand of North Beach Peninsula (Long Beach).

Upriver from Ilwaco is Megler, where ferries crossed to Astoria, Oregon, before the Astoria-Megler toll bridge was built a few years ago. This stretch of river is lined with some pleasant, quiet villages. At Cathlamet is a bridge to Puget Island, worth a visit for its gentle, pastoral scenery and small-boat moorings. The cities of Longview and Kelso, at the point of the river where it turns south toward Portland, are busy wood processing centers. At this point Interstate 5 becomes the road along the river, but alternate routes are available for those who are repelled by the robot rhythm of the multiple-lane freeway. At Longview there is a mile-and-a-half-long cantilever bridge that reaches over to Rainier, Oregon. Now the spectacular beauty of the Cascade range begins to appear as the famous volcanic Mt. St. Helens appears center stage, due east. Rugged Mt. Adams, farther east is also part of the view.

Vancouver is the first city among Washington's Columbia River towns. Another distinction: it is the oldest city in the state. Fort Vancouver was founded in 1824 by the Hudson's Bay Company. Here, the Columbia takes a straight easterly direction. Not far beyond Vancouver, the river has fashioned a showy setting on its north bank. Beacon Rock rises a sheer 850 feet above the river east of Washougal, but is easily climbed for a magnificent view of the Columbia River Gorge because of the well-engineered trail worked into its sides. The outlook to the east shows the river enfolded between its high, forested banks, with Mt. Hood in Oregon and Mt. Adams to the north posing in the wings. To the west the Columbia River islands stand out, as do the cliffs on the Oregon side of the gorge.

The next important sight upriver is Bonneville Dam, last downstream dam and first to be built on the river. This part of southern Washington encompasses the Gifford Pinchot National Forest, which includes the afore-mentioned Mt. St. Helens and Mt. Adams. A bit past the town of Stevenson, the Wind River comes tumbling out of this forest. Its course is followed for 15 miles by a paved road. A trip up this spectacular canyon brings multiple rewards, one of which is crossing the Wind River on a suspension bridge 250 feet over the stream. Another is the sight, to the north, of Mt. St. Helens, when the observer gets up high enough to look across the long stretch of forest.

Although you'd hardly know it, just a few miles east of the Wind River road, the Columbia Highway (State 14) crosses the crest of the Cascades. After the town of White Salmon, the change from west slope to east begins to show. The forest shifts from fir to pine and becomes more open. The hilly terrain turns browner. This is apple and huckleberry country: apples are grown on the hills around White Salmon, and huckleberries are found on the lower slopes of Mt. Adams, a few miles to the north.

From White Salmon, State Highway 141 heads for the recreation area around Mt. Adams. The mountain landscape is quite open, left that way many years ago after forest fires. The 12,307 foot peak has nine separate glaciers and many ice caves. One of the caves is near Trout Lake and is readily accessible. From roads that go up Mt. Adams to timberline, the hiker can easily reach the snow level for marvelous views of Mt. St. Helens and Mt. Hood. The crest of Adams, itself, seems startlingly close, but to reach it requires a long, hard climb for experienced mountaineers.

Mount St. Helens, that jewel-like mountain that sits serenely at the western edge of the Pinchot forest, recently brought fame to the Washington Cascades. On May 18, 1980, power unleashed itself from deep within the mountain. Over 1,200 feet of the mountain's top blew apart, raising a plume of gas and debris 63,000 feet above the earth. The popular Spirit Lake, located six miles from the peak, was inundated with mud, rock and ash, changing the size and dimensions. No longer did the rich timber stands reach to the sky. Everything was quickly destroyed on the north side of the mountain. Today, after much excavation, cleaning of debris, and extensive conservation work, the once popular recreation site is, again, open to the public. Life has begun anew.

Moving up the Columbia again, we reach The Dalles Dam, which holds back the Columbia to form Lake Celilo, extending 24 miles to John Day Dam. John Day, the newest dam (completed in 1968) on the lower Columbia, backs the river up 76 miles to McNary Dam, which stretches between Benton County, Washington, and Umatilla County, Oregon. Lake Umatilla, thus created, is second only in size to Roosevelt Lake on the upper Columbia. These dams and others on the river are giant power producers and bring water to otherwise arid regions. Klickitat County, stretching along the river from the east slope of the Cascades for about 70 miles, and southern Benton County next to it, have developed enormously as agricultural marketplaces since these dams were constructed on the lower Columbia.

As it has for eons, the mighty Columbia exerts a mighty control over the destiny of what is now southern Washington. Before civilized man came, the inhabitants simply marveled at the immense power of the river to shape the land as it pleased. Now man has learned to leash and manipulate for his benefit this priceless natural resource.

The Mountains

The Cascades are the mountainous barrier dividing the "wet" side from the "dry" side of Washington. The fir forests of western Washington are jungle-like, especially on the Olympic Peninsula; the eastern forests are much more open, sparse woods, mostly pine. As a unified range, the Cascades are probably unequalled in this country. The Washington Cascades are also more glaciated than any other range in the United States. Not as high as the Rockies, the Cascades are more spectacular. The Rockies stand on a mile-and-a-half-high plateau; the Cascades have their bases near sea level and rise uninterrupted 6,000 to 9,000 feet. Volcanic peaks in the range — like Mt. Baker, Glacier Peak, Mt. Rainier, Mt. Adams, and Mt. St. Helens — tower above the rest of the range. The tallest and most massive is 14,410-foot Mt. Rainier, biggest in the contiguous 48 states. A few mountains are officially taller, but they are high points on ridges. Mt. Rainier stands alone, twice as high as peaks around it.

Mt. Rainier's glaciers also set it apart. Its 26 active glaciers comprise the largest single-peak system in the continental United States. The enormous mountain can be seen for great distances north-south and east-west when the weather is right, so it is really a landmark and check point for all of Washington, and neighboring areas as well. It has been set aside as a national park and contains virgin timber whose like may never be seen again. Its slopes are carpeted with wildflowers when the snow melts, and the roads of its park cross four plant zones. Rainier creates its own climate, and with Puget Sound only 40 miles away, the interaction of the mountain's cold bulk with the moist winds from the west makes for some formidable weather. The summer months offer the best weather for exploring the mountain's various landscapes. The snow on the trails at 6,000 feet (Paradise Valley level) is usually gone by mid-July. Within the park are roads from which the mountain can be seen in its many different aspects, in addition to campgrounds, and good hiking trails from which to take closeup looks at the wilderness. There's even a guide service that takes climbing parties to Rainier's very summit, in a two-day trip.

Mt. Adams and Mt. St. Helens, to the south, have been discussed in the chapter on southern Washington. The North Cascades are left for us to define and to study. Up to very recently, no road crossed these wide and rugged peaks. Now the North Cascades Highway breaches the mountains from Diablo Dam on the west and Methow Valley on the east.

The Cascades Range is about 50-miles wide through Washington, except in the northern mountains, which are about twice that width. Glacier Peak, Mt. Baker and Mt. Shuksan are the dominant spires. Until the new highway was finished, all roads into this area were old logging or mining roads. Glacier Peak Wilderness, itself, is open only by trail. Many roads on the west and south side of the wilderness lead to low-level camping areas from which streamside trails can be followed up into the high country.

The new road across the North Cascades is the culmination of a 100-year-old dream. Fur trader Alexander Ross wrote in his diary, in 1814, of exploring these mountains. A few men like Ross, traders and trappers, were for years the only humans to venture into the rugged land. The California gold strike of 1849 excited prospectors to move northward and begin working streams through Oregon and Washington. Ruby-colored stones, found with the gold nuggets that started the rush into the North Cascades in 1858, gave Ruby Creek its name. The creek flows along the west side of the present highway (State 20), emptying into Ross Lake. The gold rush lasted only one year in the North Cascades, the primary reason for its brevity being the hardships and difficult access problems posed by this primitive area. Another short-lived flurry of gold fever struck about 20 years later, when gold was found in the headwaters of the Skagit River. This, too, was doomed by lack of transportation. Miners and cattlemen in the Okanogan Valley began around this time to petition the legislature of the new state for help in getting their products to market. In 1893 the legislators appropriated $20,000 to build 200 miles of road from Bellingham

Bay to the Columbia River via Ruby Creek — $100 a mile for a road through what is probably the most rugged section of the United States. In 1896 a wagon road was started from Marblemount along the Cascade River. The following year it was impassable because of slides and washouts. The road was extended almost to Cascade Pass in the 1930s.

The North Cross State Highway Association, a group organized in the 1950s, was primarily responsible for the eventual completion of the cross-mountain road. The final route, begun in 1960, was up Ruby, Granite, and Early Winters creeks.

Some of the breathtaking scenery along the new road includes the Ross Lake National Recreation area and its three lakes — Gorge, Diablo, and Ross — strung out along the highway. These are lakes formed by the Skagit River Hydroelectric Project, furnishing power to the city of Seattle. Diablo Lake is especially beautiful with its blue-green color that results from the fine sediment carried to it by streams coming out of glaciers. Ross Dam, 540 feet high is the tallest of the three dams in the project.

The "eternal snows" of the Cascades, and especially the North Cascades, are caused by the enormous snow packs — 20-feet deep in the higher elevations — accumulated during the season of snowfall. Avalanches sometimes isolate mountain communities here during the winter months. The glaciers and icy spires of these mountains are the remnant of the last ice age 10,000 years ago, which created the area's alpine scenery — U-shaped valleys, horns, serrated ridges, hanging valleys, and cirque or tarn lakes. This is really glacier country: of the 1,100 glaciers in the continental United States, Washington has 800.

Even the most fearsomely rugged parts of the earth can be quite fragile. Now that the North Cascades have been opened to relatively easy access, more and more people will be able to motor into that mountain fastness and find rejuvenation of spirit at a relatively low cost in terms of effort. This may not be all to the good. An old axiom observes that whatever is to be truly appreciated is not won without a struggle. But let us assume that we have grown up enough so that the corollary of the axiom need not apply, to wit: what man obtains with ease he is quick to despoil.

Central Washington

The "east slope" is the central part of Washington, distinct from the western valleys and the extreme east. It runs all the way from the Canadian border to Oregon on the south. With the Cascades on one side and the Columbia River on the other, this central strip has managed very well to be neither beholden to Seattle or Spokane and their spheres. Its cities are thriving centers for the agricultural prosperity of the farmlands and orchards of the central valleys. Yakima, Ellensburg, Wenatchee, Chelan, and Okanogan supply not only Washington but the whole country with fruit and produce. The famous Washington apples are sent all over the world from this area. The dams on the middle Columbia and on the Yakima River have been crucial to the fairly recent agricultural exploitation of this part of the state. The Columbia dams have, in addition, made ports again out of these inland towns. Not only has this been accomplished, but the great amounts of power supplied by the dams have increased the area's industrial potential.

In north central Washington, there is no clearly defined boundary where the east slope of the Cascades leaves off. The mountains just go on, never subsiding into plains or valleys, except for the narrow Okanogan Valley, a wild yet hospitable country popular as a summer resort area. This area of the central belt, reaching south to the Columbia and north to the border, is called the Okanogan Highlands. The great river's east-west course in this part of the state ends at Pateros, where the Columbia turns south and is joined by the Methow River, whose pastoral valley leads up into the high northern Cascades.

One of the most remarkable features of north-central Washington is Lake Chelan, a natural lake lying in a glacial trough whose lower end was dammed up long ago by a colossal terminal moraine. The lake is 60 miles long, and the translation of its Indian name is "deep water." A depth of 1,600 feet has been recorded for the lake. A passenger- and mail-carrying ferry makes a daily trip from Chelan at the lower end to Stehekin 55 miles away at the head of the lake. Visitors can ride all the way or be put ashore at one of the many isolated campgrounds along the way. In the summer months a Forest Service ranger goes along and describes points of interest to passengers. The town of Stehekin can be reached only by boat, seaplane, or foot trail over the Cascades. It is set amid a sumptuous alpine landscape whose jagged peaks are 8,500 to 9,500 feet high and still relatively anonymous to everyone but those dedicated recreationists who have fought hard to preserve this region in its natural state. The Lake Chelan National Recreation Area was established by Congress with the specific prohibition against the construction of roads from the outside world to the Stehekin Valley.

Wenatchee sits in mid-state between the north-south borders. Its big-money crop is apples. Its apple orchards line up on both sides of the Columbia and a long way up the Wenatchee River valley. The hardy Winesap and Delicious varieties grown here have a special "bite" that makes them great eating apples, and a "build" that insures long-lasting quality. That's why they can be shipped all over the globe. The Wenatchee Apple Blossom Festival has become a traditional celebration as well as a tourist attraction.

Yakima is the largest and still the most booming of the east-slope cities. It may not have as famous a rodeo as Ellensburg, 37 miles north on US 97, but it is the hub of the Yakima Valley, an area of immense importance economically and becoming more so. A good idea of the valley's riches can be obtained by taking a loop trip from Yakima to Prosser along the Yakima River, returning on the other side of the river. Along the way are lush fruit orchards, fields of produce, hop yards, and vineyards, and it is possible to purchase (or even pick) produce right from the field. At Cherry Hill, near Granger, there is a panoramic and detailed view of the lower valley. Yakima celebrates the climax of harvest season with the Central Washington fair late in September.

Ellensburg's rodeo is a logical reflection of its situation on the plains, where both horses and alfalfa are raised. East of Ellensburg near Vantage, on the

Columbia's bank, is the Ginkgo Petrified Forest. It was formed when lava invaded a lake full of watersoaked ginkgo logs. Mineral deposits gradually replaced wood fiber, turning the logs into stone. A museum on the site illustrates how all this happened.

Horse Heaven Hills, between the Yakima Valley and the Columbia River, is a formerly arid region that has become prosperous in recent times because of increased rainfall. It is a rather remote area where wild horses used to roam, and some of them still do, it is said. The hills rise higher and higher as they stretch from the river west through the Yakima Indian Reservation toward the Cascades.

The central Washington belt seems an obvious receiving area for the expanding number of people who have lately "discovered" the Northwest. Its mild climate and lush, protected valleys invite settlement. But one hopes it won't come about in so massive a tide that the east slope valleys become any less desirable as dwelling places.

Eastern Washington

The catchy term, "Inland Empire," is used to mean any part of the country within Spokane's sphere of influence. This takes in parts of Idaho, Montana, and Oregon, as well as eastern Washington. Spokane claims all of Washington from the Cascade slope east, but since the central belt has become an economic entity of its own, able to ship directly to its markets, Spokane's influence has diminished somewhat so far as Washington is concerned.

The *real* eastern side of Washington, roughly the dividing line where the Columbia River winds through the state, is in night-and-day contrast to the "wet half" west of the Cascades. The central belt has this difference too, but in a milder way. The Columbia Basin lands between that river and the Snake in the southeast would be close to pure desert were it not for the gigantic system of dams on these two rivers in Washington. The eastern lands used to be typical "Wild West," with endless stretches of dry, open spaces, cattle ranges, and wheat fields, with considerable mining activity in the mountains to the north. But Grand Coulee and the lesser Basin projects have changed all that, if not in substance at least in emphasis. Agriculture is now about as varied as anywhere in the country, and many of the tiny villages in these parts have grown up into good-sized cities.

Spokane, as the hub of its "empire," has benefitted most from the various irrigation and hydroelectric projects. It has become the second city in Washington and, as an expression of its new eminence, mounted an extraordinarily successful world's fair — Expo 74 — in 1974. But Spokane's growth has escaped much of the uglification that seems to be an adjunct of city growth. The beautiful and turbulent Spokane River, which cuts through the city, is kept as nearly as possible the way nature made it. At 5,514-acre Riverside State Park near the city, the river rushes through a lava gorge shaded by pines. Within a 50-mile radius of Spokane are 76 lakes, most with gently sloping beaches and some thrusting watery fingers back into the hills.

Mt. Spokane, 34 miles northeast, is in the center of a 24,000-acre state park, Washington's largest. The mountain, 5,800 feet high, is a popular skiing area and from its summit can be seen mountains and lakes in Washington, Idaho and Montana. Fishing and hunting for game animals, which include deer, elk, and even bear, are excellent in this area. Although Spokane has been tamed since the days when it was the whoop-it-up place for miners, ranchers and construction workers, it hasn't lost the color and individuality of its beginnings in its rise to big-city status.

The Columbia Basin includes just about all of eastern Washington except the mountainous regions in the north. Uncounted millions of years ago, during a period of many centuries, molten rock poured over a volcanic landscape in central and eastern Washington. Then glaciers came, melted, and wore coulees, or canyons, in the volcanic layers. The biggest hollow was Grand Coulee. The waters from the last ice age created a giant river, the forerunner of the present-day Columbia. In volume it would make today's great river seem insignificant by comparison. When the glacial torrent receded and the Columbia settled into its bed, vast areas of the rich, volcanic soil were left dry. Until the Columbia Basin Reclamation Project was completed, the potential of the region for supporting human populations was untapped. The monumental dam that is the key to Basin irrigation, Grand Coulee Dam, is 550 feet high and 4,175 feet long. Canals and reservoirs carry its impounded waters far and wide.

The colossal lake created by Grand Coulee Dam stretches 150 miles from the dam to the Canadian border. Its 660 miles of shoreline are included within the Coulee Dam National Recreation Area. From the north end of Roosevelt Lake, a scenic trip can be made, encompassing a river valley called the Sanpoil, whose gentle aspect is a startling contrast to the Roosevelt Lake area and coulee country. The valley can be reached by the Sherman Creek road (State Highway 30) west from Kettle Falls, crossing Sherman Pass, the highest in Washington. From the pass there are views of Roosevelt Lake on the east and south and the

Okanogan Highlands and Cascades to the west. State Highway 21 is taken heading south from the town of Republic, following the narrow river valley, with its pine forests and farmlands.

The coulee country is in the heart of eastern Washington. It is a region of geological wonders — old lava flows, dry river beds, and fossil caves. Dry Falls State Park, south of Grand Coulee, provides an illustration. Dry Falls is believed to have been one of the greatest falls ever formed. From a vantage point in the park can be seen the five huge recesses or alcoves over which the water flowed, dropping 400 feet over an extent of 3-1/2 miles. The desert country below Dry Falls has natural lakes that occur in a 20-mile stretch of the lower coulee and help make the area one of eastern Washington's most popular vacation spots. It's a land full of strange formations, odd rocks, and other things that make life pleasant for geologists.

Irrigation has spread south from Coulee Dam and created farmlands out of what was once millions of acres of desert. In the many coulees that cut into these plains can be seen millions of years of geologic time. Inspection of these layers is especially easy to do by car on State Highway 155, which follows Grand Coulee.

At the town of Moses Lake, a bit to the south, is a splendid museum that describes and illustrates with specimens the history and geology of the region. Just a little farther to the south is Potholes Reservoir, created by O'Sullivan Dam, and filling a whole valley with its vast waters.

The southeast corner of Washington is a land of bleak vistas, deep chasms, and arid mountains, a stretch of end-of-the-world landscape whose character is emphasized by the deep gorge of Hell's Canyon to the east, and the swift-flowing Snake River rushing through it .The Blue Mountains dominate the region that borders Oregon, spreading across the line into that state. Service roads are the only ones that penetrate the lonely fastnesses of the Blue Mountains, although there is a 263-mile highway loop around them, including the Oregon segment. A dirt road that crosses these mountains from Dayton to Tollgate, Oregon, is driveable only in summer. From Asotin, near the Idaho border, a dirt road follows the Snake for a while, but turns away toward the

78

Grande Ronde where that river comes up from Oregon. The north leg of US Highway 12, from Walla Walla to Clarkston, roughly follows the route of the Snake, skirting the Blue Mountains and passing through some peaceful little towns that used to be swingers when they were on the stagecoach route and entertained miners and gamblers. Lewis and Clark passed this way, and some of the places along the road claim honors as places where the celebrated explorers stopped over, including Lewis and Clark Trail State Park between Waitsburg and Dayton.

Walla Walla (an Indian name meaning "many waters") began as a boom town. It was a base for gold prospectors on their way to Idaho in the 1860s. Nowadays, it is an agricultural center with a big canning industry, growing primarily wheat and peas. Whitman College, the oldest in the state, is at Walla Walla. The Whitman Mission, established in 1836, is nearby. It was a haven for migrants traveling over the Oregon Trail in the earlier days of the westward movement. Traffic into Washington ceased around mid-century as wagon trains began heading more directly to the Willamette Valley in Oregon. The Whitmans and others of the mission were massacred by Indians in the wars of the fifties.

The Indian wars broke out in earnest after a peace treaty had been signed in 1855. Colonel Steptoe and some troops from Walla Walla had marched north to the area of a butte 30 miles south of a trading post later to become Spokane. The Indians, encamped on the butte, had visual command of the whole Palouse country and saw him coming. The colonel and his men were soundly thrashed. Oddly, the infamous butte was later named for the colonel. Steptoe Butte, near the town of Rosalie, rises 3,600 feet above the plateau. It is an ancient mountain whose top was untouched by the lava flows that spread over the Columbia Basin after the mountain had formed. Steptoe, by the way, fared better than Custer did some years later. He and his men were surrounded on a hill but managed to slip across the Snake River at night when the overconfident Indians relaxed their guard, intending to finish off the troops the next day.

For a time the Snake was considered by both sides as the boundary line for settlers, but when gold was found in Idaho, hordes of whites poured in by land and by river. Steamboats charged up the Snake to Lewiston, then up the

Clearwater River. In later days the Snake was the prime route for transporting wheat, which was lowered by tramway over cliffs some 2,000 feet high to barges in the canyons northeast of Pomeroy.

The Palouse River cuts an impressive figure through this country. On the way to its junction with the Snake, it has carved a deep canyon of its own, one feature of which is Palouse Falls, dropping 198 feet into the canyon.

The "other-world" contrasts that are scattered through much of eastern Washington may impart a valuable lesson to us by reason of their strangeness, a lesson in the capacity of nature for infinite variety. In the natural realm, all things can be and often are replaced, and in their stead arises a new creation sometimes vastly different from and superior to the one that had existed. We may well ponder the evidence.